CHATTO
CounterBlasts

Christopher
HITCHENS

The Monarchy

Chatto & Windus
LONDON

314779
354. 41 HIT
POLITICS
MONARCH   UK
BRITISH MONARCHY

Published in 1990 by
Chatto & Windus Ltd
20 Vauxhall Bridge Road
London SW1V 2SA

A CIP catalogue record for this book
is available from the British Library

ISBN 0 7011 3555 7

Photoset in Linotron Ehrhardt by
Rowland Phototypesetting Ltd
Bury St Edmunds, Suffolk
Printed in Great Britain by
St Edmundsbury Press Ltd
Bury St Edmunds, Suffolk

The Monarchy

NIGHT IS COMING on, and the urgent, meretricious tones of the television news muzak are heard. We know that this strident, bombastic noise is a subliminal appeal to think of 'news' as part drama, part sensation and part entertainment (like the fanfares from the telescreen in Orwell's dystopia) but we are won over to give it another chance. What is being heralded by this racket, this time? It might be fire, flood or famine; assassination or invasion; coup or communiqué. Is it just tomorrow's talking point, or is it one of those events that stay imprinted on the memory for good? Well, neither actually. On the evening I'm thinking of, the first and longest bulletin from a potential world of agony and ecstasy was one which sounded a false alarm. The Queen Mother had been incommoded by a morsel of food wedged in her throat.

What *is* this? Why, when the subject of royalty or monarchy is mentioned, do the British bid adieu to every vestige of proportion, modesty, humour and restraint? Why, in this dubious and sentimental cause, will they even abandon their claim to a stiff upper lip? We read with revulsion about those countries where the worship of mediocre individuals – the Ceauşescu dynasty in Romania comes to mind – has become even more of an offence than it has a bore. We are supposed to know enough to recoil from sickly adulation, and from its counterpart, which is hypocrisy and envy. We learn from history the subtle and deadly damage that is done to *morale* by the alternation between sycophancy and resentment. Yet the unwholesome cult of the Windsors and the Waleses is beginning to turn morbid before our eyes.

'Either at your throat or at your feet.' So runs the old maxim about Fleet Street. Fair-weather in its affections, and with a shrewd eye for the 'market forces' in opinion that have become a secular religion, the mouthpieces of the New Britain trade on love and hate by debasing and cheapening both. At one moment, the affected, stifling hush of reverence that attends the Mountbatten funeral or the politicised 'let's pretend' that is the Queen's Speech to Parliament. At another, the agonising fixity of the grin as the minor sprigs of the Royal House do their turn on *It's a Knockout*. In between, the mock-seriousness and the frowning, stupid non-questions about non-subjects. Has Princess Diana grown up? Does Prince Charles know enough about architecture? Should the Queen abdicate? Is the monarchy too remote? Is it remote *enough*?

This symbiosis between the sacred and the profane and the noble and the vulgar is an embarrassing sign of underdevelopment. As a homage to antiquity and tradition it is a cringe-making failure. As an exercise in bread and circuses it is a flop. As the invisible cement to a system of supposedly well-ordered and historically-evolved democracy, it looks more and more like the smirk on the corpse. It has led to a most un-English impasse, where a Poujadiste female with ideas above her station has appropriated the regal 'We' and many of Its prerogatives, and where a middlebrow Prince of the Blood mutters worriedly about the torn and worn fabric of society and its contract. Things are so distempered and out of joint, in fact, that sturdy democrats, even including a few born-again Monarchist-Leninists, are sighing for the piping times of the past.

Yet, if we ask how we got here from there, we will discover that the institution of monarchy, and the dull habits of mind that are inseparable from it, are themselves part of the difficulty. The monarchy may now be compromising with its own faint, puzzled, insipid impression of 'image' and modernity, and looking foolish and undignified into the bargain. But the inescapable question – 'do we need a monarchy in the first place or at all?' – has at last been asked. Let us try for a polite but firm reply.

The English have long been convinced that they are admired and envied by the rest of the world for their eccentricities alone. Many of these eccentricities – red telephone boxes with heavy doors, unarmed policemen, courtesy in sporting matters – are now more durable as touristic notions than as realities. But there is one special and distinc-

3

tive feature of the island race which remains un-
altered. Neither the English/British nor their
foreign admirers and rivals know quite what the
country is called.

Most nations, ancient and modern, have an agreed
name. But we do not know whether this nation
inhabits England, Britain, the British Isles, Albion
or the UK. The only accurate nomenclature is the
one that nobody employs – 'the United Kingdom
of Great Britain and Northern Ireland'. The words
express the hope of a political and historical compromise rather than the actuality of one. If it were to read
'The United *State* of Great Britain and Northern
Ireland' it would provoke unfeeling mirth. And the
United *Republic* would sound positively grotesque.
No, it is the word 'kingdom' that lends the tone. The
British actually define their country and implicitly
their society as, first and last, *a monarchy*.

This fact is so salient that people are apt to miss it.
The ruling party forms Her Majesty's Government
and the opposition parties make up Her Majesty's
Loyal Opposition. The right people speak the
Queen's English (though mercifully few employ her
tone). The Queen's peace is kept, at least so far as
the defence of the *realm* goes, by the Royal Navy
and the Royal Air Force and any number of royally-
commissioned regiments. No letter or parcel may
be sent without a royal endorsement in the form of a
Queen's head. The adjective 'royal' is an automatic
enhancer, with the Fleet Street usage 'right royal'

4

meaning anything that is extra or jolly good, most especially if it involves royal patronage or the royal warrant as in the bizarre, cumbersome re-naming of the 'Royal' National Theatre.

Satirising the credulity and the servility of the English/British over a century ago, William Cobbett remarked that you could tell a lot about a country which referred to the *Royal* Mint and the *National* Debt. Indeed, the attachment to royalty has more than a dash of the religious about it. Just as the holy men will tell us to thank god for our many blessings and to put the many things that are *not* blessings down to the undoubted fact that god moves in a mysterious way, so the monarchy is praised and extolled for all the honourable and admirable aspects of the country which it symbolises, while avoiding even a whisper of blame for anything that might have gone, or be going, amiss. This process is given a palpable fillip by the fact that the Queen is head of the state church and styles herself 'defender of the faith'. As the then Archbishop of Canterbury quite unaffectedly remarked on the occasion of the present Queen's coronation: 'This country and Commonwealth last Tuesday were not far from the Kingdom of Heaven.' Some critics of the monarchy, perhaps seeking to give a demotic and levelling flavour to their outlandish and usually ignored reservations, have foolishly stressed the large private holdings in land, property and specie which are enjoyed by the

Crown and added to by the Civil List. This is to miss the point. There is an all-important sense in which the Crown possesses the entire country, from its devotions to its most secular observances, and makes the British the last people in the modern world to be subject to the authentic forms of monarchy. An anthropologist observing our tribe for the first time would be bound to note a strongly marked and continuous adherence, in the first place to a fetish, and in the second place to a taboo on the discussion of it. This pamphlet may not be able to do anything about the fetish, but it does hope to do something about the taboo.

Fetish and taboo need not automatically imply mystery. There is nothing very puzzling, on the face of it, in the British people's unembarrassed love for, and pride in, monarchy. It was once said of the use of cavalry in modern warfare that it lent tone and dash to what would otherwise be a vulgar brawl, and the royal spectacle is an element of colour in a canvas that often seems in sore need of it.

The British also make more history than they can consume locally, and to many people it seems that the monarch is the living emblem of a considerable past. By the sort of subliminal effect that overseas British Tourist Board campaigns are so good at bringing off, the idea of the Palace and the Coach is commingled with Shakespeare, Dickens, the country house, the castle, the paintings of Constable and the choir of King's College Chapel, to form a reassuring, organic and pleasing whole. Even those who know this effect to be misleading and indiscriminate are not wholly proof against its allure.

Then, it is fair to say, there is the personality of Our Sovereign Lady herself. She is a decent and dignified woman to all outward appearances, with a strong sense of duty, an abiding fondness for animals and a preference for life's less complicated pleasures. Who knows what instinct was at work when the wives of striking coal-miners decided to by-pass what they thought to be a callous government and petition the Queen directly? The implied compliment to her sense of fair play made a more lasting impression than any reciprocal gesture on her part could have done, and testified to the extreme sturdiness of the roots of populist monarchism.

Let us then, take the monarchy at its strongest, admit its genuine appeal and begin with the present overwhelmingly popular reign.

Shortly before the Queen's Jubilee in 1977, Paul Johnson, who might without offence to himself be described as one of Her Majesty's Journalists, wrote a loyalist essay describing Elizabeth II as 'Head of Her Profession'. In the first year of her succession, he pointed out:

> The Tories had just got back to office after the Attlee years; Churchill had made his famous address to Congress, Monty was at NATO HQ, Stalin ruled Russia, Chiang's men were fighting a

7

rearguard action against the Chinese Communists on the Burma frontier. Virtually the whole of Africa was still partitioned among the colonial powers, and the British authorities had just informed the UN that they did not see their way to abolishing flogging in the mandated territories.

Not exactly the Kingdom of Heaven, perhaps, but from some interested viewpoints not at all bad. One could add to this that in 1952 the pound sterling was worth the better part of four dollars, that *The Times* newspaper was *The Times* newspaper, that the four provinces of the United Kingdom were untroubled by thoughts of schism, that the Metropolitan Police were thought to be incorruptible, that the Church of England was unmolested by doubts, that the Universities of Oxford and Cambridge were as renowned for their high and objective standards as was the British Broadcasting Corporation, that the Lords and Commons enjoyed a harmonious consensus on governance, that the long age of Butskellism was about to dawn, that most of those who wished for work could find it and that most non-white British passport holders lived beyond the seas.

Look first upon that picture, and on this . . . In the course of the present reign, or 'the second Elizabethan era' as it was bravely hailed in 1952 and at the Coronation the following year, the country has passed through a staggering declension. Even the famed political energy and ruthlessness

8

of the Thatcher decade may come to be seen by historians as an episode in that decline rather than as the counter to it.

Of the nation's institutions, only one still enjoys anything like the status that it possessed when the present reign began. And even some partisans of that one institution – which is of course the Royal Family – have worried that there may be something hysterical; something un-*English* almost, in the adulation which this family receives wherever it goes and whatever it does. Might the adulation perhaps have something to do with a queasy, half-conscious fear that, shorn of the monarchy, we should have to confront all these other decaying institutions unconsoled; *alone*? If this suspicion is warranted, then the orb and the sceptre have become actual obstacles to clear sight; have come to substitute for a vacancy. The tribe that confuses its totems and symbols with reality has succumbed to fetishism and may be in more trouble than it realises.

It is generally possible to tell, in English arguments, when a taboo is being broken. An important early warning will be people starting to say very loudly that such and such a subject 'isn't really that important'. This is what Edmund Wilson, writing in 1945, termed our national weakness for 'the False Issue':

This is best handled in the tone of light ridicule. They acquire the technique so early that I think

9

they must be trained in it at Oxford. If you do not want to stand by the Poles, you make fun of them for their effervescence, thus implying that they are quite irresponsible; if Gandhi is becoming too powerful, you are amusing about his loin-cloth and goat. Only in more aggravated cases do you resort to moral indignation.

The monarchy counts as an aggravated case, all right. The first False Issue one normally encounters is the claim that it has 'no real power'. One never quite knows what 'real' is intended to mean here, but the conventions of the False Issue lead one to guess that the word is doing duty for 'formal'. Thus is the red herring introduced. A moment later, the same speaker is telling another listener of all the good things that the monarchy is a 'force' for. These good things invariably turn out to be connected to power. They are things like 'stability', 'unity', 'national cohesion', 'continuity' and other things for which powerless people would find it difficult to be a force. Edmund Wilson would have had little trouble noticing, furthermore, that all the above good things are keywords for conservative and establishment values.

Here, for example, are all the things that Her Majesty's Ministers may do by means of an exercise of the Royal Prerogative, without choosing to make themselves accountable to the Commons or to the voters:

1. Make Orders in Council
2. Declare War
3. Make Peace
4. Recognise foreign governments
5. Sign and ratify treaties
6. Grant pardons
7. Grant charters
8. Confer honours
9. Confer patronage appointments
10. Establish commissions.

This list is not exhaustive, but nor is it a record of impotence. It might, but probably won't, give pause to those who imagine that the monarchy and its functions are purely decorative and ceremonial. It could also give pause to those neo-monarchists who argue, oozing democratic precept from every pore, that the monarchy in England is a guarantee against unchecked political power; against executive or elective dictatorship. In point of fact the very opposite is the case. The prerogative of the Crown; the enthronement of 'The Crown in Parliament', is the special and particular symbol of our status as subjects instead of citizens. It is a rubbing in of the fact that we have no rights, properly understood, but rather traditions that depend on the caprice of a political compromise made in 1688.

During the 1988 tercentary of that 'Glorious Revolution' which buckled the present phase of English monarchy into position, there were a number of commemorative and celebratory events. One of these took the form of an exhibition in the Banqueting House in Whitehall, with mobile wax-works to show King William of Orange and Queen Mary mounting a very British coup, and the other brought the Queen herself to Westminster Hall to preside over a 'Loyal' address from both Houses. Only the correspondent of the *Independent* noticed that, for this latter occasion, a small velvet curtain had been drawn across the plaque which records that, in Westminster Hall, King Charles I stood trial for his life.

Back up the road at the Banqueting House – where King Charles I had actually lost his life a short while after – matters were not much more honestly confronted. The lavishly-mounted exhi-bition contained no mention of the Battle of the Boyne, at which King William asserted his Protestant revolution and its power over the Irish and thus bequeathed a legacy of the most majestic kind. A parallel Dutch exhibit in The Hague, which had also been opened by Her Majesty the Queen, had given extensive space to this inescapable aspect of the Glorious Revolution. But in loyalist London – nothing. Michael Crick of Channel Four News was the only reporter to notice this piece of histori-cal fakery, and to question the curator of the exhi-bition about it. For his pains, he received a peerlessly blimpish answer. He was told that we were commemorating the 1688 revolution, and that the Boyne had been fought in 1689. Not my period, old man – philistinism in the service of deference.

These two episodes of airbrushing raise another question about the wholesomeness of the Windsor cult. Does the unruffled, unquestioning fealty to monarchy mean that we cannot look our own history in the face? The obsequious concealment of the plaque, and the dishonest omission of the origins of the Irish crisis, took place at a time when even in the Soviet Union and Poland a whole series of hitherto unmentionable events were being revived for scrutiny, analysis and consideration. Many courageous historians and scholars in those countries had endeavoured for decades to establish the right to an objective open-minded reading of the past. But in Britain – nothing that would compromise the magic of monarchy.

It isn't even necessary to assert the obvious here; that without Oliver Cromwell there might well not have been a Parliament to which Our Sovereign Lady might make her gracious address. (Until the mid 1960s, admittedly, the Palace of Westminster was a royal palace, and the chamberlains thereof could and did stop elected Members from coming into the building outside 'working hours'.) The point is simply that the execution of King Charles I did take place, that it was a hinge event in our history, and that it was seen fit politely to obliterate this fact for the purposes of a staged celebration of 'The Crown in Parliament'. Those who say that without the monarchy Britain would be a banana republic are closing their eyes to the banana republic features which the cult of monarchy necessitates. Dazzled by the show, moreover, they may be missing other long-run tendencies towards banana-dom which it is the partial function of monarchy to obscure.

We used to be more honest about this latter point. When Walter Bagehot wrote his turgid but essential study of that mythical and invisible beast, 'The English Constitution', he was good enough to divide the role of institutions into two, according to how they were, respectively, 'dignified' and 'efficient'. He expressed himself in terms which those who admired his strategy must have also felt were a little too frank:

> As long as the human heart is strong and the human reason weak, royalty will be strong because it appeals to diffuse feeling, and Republics weak because they appeal to the understanding.
>
> A secret prerogative is an anomaly – perhaps the greatest of anomalies. That secrecy is, however, essential to the utility of English royalty as it now is. Above all things our royalty is to be reverenced, and if you begin to poke about it you cannot reverence it. When there is a select committee on the Queen, the charm of royalty will be gone. Its mystery is its life. We must not let in daylight upon magic.

This comes perilously close to Lady Bracknell's rec-ommendation of the beauty of ignorance – 'Like a delicate exotic fruit; touch it, and the bloom is gone.' But notice Bagehot's sudden use, in this torrent of sickly mysticism, of the businesslike word 'utility'. He practically founded the *Economist* after all, and did not believe in something for nothing. The point of the dignified is to give an *appearance* of grandeur to mere efficiency, and to distract attention from the many lapses to which mere efficiency is prone. He might as well have come right out with it and recommended monarchy as the opiate of the people.

Note how poorly Bagehot's thesis, which is the founding document of our 'constitutional mon-archy', has worn with time. The human heart is still pretty much as strong as it was, and the human reason has not become any stronger (indeed, under the influence of monarchic hysteria it seems some-times to evaporate like a gas for whole weeks at a time) but the alternation between these two human qualities has not been much affected by a sudden and general outbreak of republics. Where once the kin of the Battenbergs could style themselves Kaiser and Czar (which are cognate with Shah and Caesar) there may since have been unanointed despots but even these have given way to the concept of citizenship and constitutional government. During the twenty-five years that King George V exercised the prerogative, five emperors, eight kings and eighteen minor dynasties expired. The British Crown survived by mutating Battenberg to Mountbatten, adopting the sound and bucolic title of 'Windsor' with its reassuring echo, and generally taking the active interest in social peace that has licensed more than one of its interventions into politics.

From this very ancestry, of course, descends the present idiom of royal interference in current debate. The stupider sort of conservative monarchist feels peeved at the fact that these discreet nudges from Palace quarters always have something – well – *compassionate* and *caring* about them. Her Majesty lets it be understood that she is concerned about South Africa and the 'New Commonwealth'. Prince Charles elongates an already long face when afflicting himself and others with worry about the ecology, the inner cities and the eternal 'problems of youth'. Rather like the defection of a segment of the Church of England and Oxbridge, this strikes the possessing classes as a piece of wanton irresponsibility and (after all we've *done* for them) ingratitude also. But it is perfectly irrelevant to any discussion of the *principle* of monarchy; as irrelevant as the notoriously authoritarian views of Prince Philip or the fabled inability of the new Princesses to keep any one thought in their heads for as long as a minute at a time. Generally speaking, the monarchy has an interest in emollience and social peace and consensus. Do we? If so, do we need to acquire the habits of acceptance and consensus by way of example from a hereditary 'fount'?

Our class system – another source of constant fascination for foreign visitors – is also based rather on the hereditary principle. And, while monarchy is not directly responsible for this delicious if disreputable fact, it is hard to imagine the social pyramid enduring as long as it has without a crown at the apex. The practice of marrying the generally foreign-born royal family into the native aristocracy, which originated with Queen Victoria and was continued (despite many predictions to the contrary) by the present heir to the throne, has also done something to cement the identification of royalty with the upper crust. There is a slight fashion, among very posh people indeed, to look down at the Windsors as a bit dumpy and bourgeois – which they most indubitably are – but this affectation is more than anything a sign of supreme confidence. The whole boneyard of Debrett and Burke, the Lords Temporal and Spiritual, the twice-annual embarrassment of the Honours List and the amazing power of patronage appointments to keep the civil service, the armed forces and the superannuated politicians and businessmen reasonably 'sweet': all this would look tawdry and corrupt if it were not sanctified by the mystery of the Crown. It is the ghost in our machine; and the desire not to disturb or profane the ghost has rescued the machine from some awkward inspections, not to say overhauls.

In his important work on authority, Max Weber distinguished three ways in which it could be manifested and exercised. The first was 'traditional'; custom-bound and hallowed by the immemorial. The second was 'legal'; founded on the ties of contract. The third was 'charismatic'; exerted by the magic or unique gifts of a single leader or ruler. In their attitude to the monarchy, the British seem to have got these three, especially the first and the second, badly confused. Our monarchy is expected both to embody the whole tradition of 'the nation' as refracted through the theme of kingship, the hedge of divinity and all the rest of it, *and* to supply the thrill of charisma. It is this latest efflorescence of the cult of Windsordom that has begun to worry even its supporters; the near-hysterical adulation and ballyhoo about everything, from the disco Princesses to the banal details of family stress (on bad days) and family reproduction (on good ones). The effect of this on a national press already heavily infected with cretinism has disturbed those who might be called 'thoughtful Establishment circles', and also some of those in and around the Court itself, who are in the awkward position of both soliciting servile publicity and recoiling from it.

Publicity, too, used to have its 'utility'. As Benjamin Disraeli, Bagehot's cynical contemporary, wrote to Matthew Arnold, 'Everyone likes flattery; and when you come to Royalty you should lay it on with a trowel'. Early manifestations of royal fever were in fact exactly that; Queen Victoria at the bedside of the typhoid-stricken Prince of Wales in 1871 was a perfect image of glutinous sentimentality perfectly apt for the age. Later experiences with royal appendectomy were to give huge helpings of raw material to the early years of Fleet Street as it began its long and ultimately successful quest for the lowest common denominator. If the Palace press office now regrets its collusion with this process, it's too late. But it's unlikely that the paradox of collusion between the hereditary and the vulgar in Britain will soon disappear. It has been too important a mainstay of reaction down the generations to be lightly jettisoned because it is in danger of 'going too far'.

These, then, are the headings for a critique. The British monarchy inculcates unthinking credulity and servility. It forms a heavy layer on the general encrustation of our unreformed political institutions. It is the gilded peg from which our unlovely system of social distinction and hierarchy depends. It is an obstacle to the objective public discussion of our own history. It tribalises politics. It entrenches the absurdity of the hereditary principle. It contributes to what sometimes looks like an enfeeblement of the national intelligence, drawing from our press and even from some of our poets the sort of degrading and abnegating propaganda that would arouse contempt if displayed in Zaire or Romania. It is, in short, neither dignified nor efficient.

What are the objections to this critique? They are all formulated in terms of some or all of the following:

1. The Royal Family provides continuity and stability.
2. The Royal Family provides glamour and pageantry.
3. The Royal Family does not interfere in politics, but lends tone to it.
4. The Royal Family is preferable to the caprices of presidential government.
5. The Royal Family is a guarantee of the national 'identity'.

If we take these in order, we find a thicket of tautology and contradiction. Argument (1) is congruent with arguments (2) and (5) but is in flat opposition to arguments (3) and (4). So the order of reply and rebuttal is necessarily a bit ragged. Nevertheless:

1. **Continuity and stability** Well, up to a point. It would be equally true and one-sided to say that British history or English history is a series of violent ruptures and upheavals over the struggle for the throne. At some point in the relatively recent past, we ceased to periodise history by reigns and began to do so by decades. Both periodisations are arbitrary, but the number of times that a royal

'succession' has been peaceful or has resulted in 'stability' is relatively few. Between the execution of King Charles I outside the Banqueting House in January 1649, for example, and the extinction of the Jacobite cause at Culloden in 1746, not even Thomas Hobbes himself could make complete sense of the monarchic principle. It kept having to be reinvented by force, and needed repeated infusions from already etiolated European mainland princelings. Even after the Hanoverians achieved grudging acceptance, which they did principally in the making of national and patriotic wars in the American colonies and against revolutionary and then Bonapartist France, and finally against their own Teutonic cousins, there were some shocks. It's not considered all that polite to dwell on the fact, but only an exercise of laughable moral absolutism in 1936 prevented (by accident admittedly, but then all things predicated on the hereditary principle are by accident) the accession of a young man with a pronounced sympathy for National Socialism. The former Edward VIII, as Duke of Windsor, was a permanent worry and embarrassment to the British government during the Second World War, and seems never to have abandoned his conviction that Hitler had a point. Had things gone the other way, he was a candidate for providing stability and continuity to a foreign-imposed régime of quite a different sort.

2. **Glamour and pageantry** No country or form of government can ever quite do without this, and the British are fortunate in having a certain amount to spare. Whether you find them charming or boring, the May morning singers at Magdalen Tower or the Durham miners' gala or the Morris Dancers or the Beating of the Bounds are lodged in the national routine and represent a long and varied history as well as the ingrained human instinct for ceremony. (Any country, too, must find a way to commemorate its fallen, though presumably some of the younger Windsors must wince a bit when they see 'For King and Country' written so accusingly, and so *accurately* on the granite obelisks that keep green the memory of the Somme.)

The thing about the royalist contribution to national ritual, by contrast, is the amount of contrivance and greasepaint that it has required and does require. The classic instance of invented tradition is probably the astonishingly bogus episode of the 'Investiture' of the Prince of Wales. Tom Nairn has caught the fraudulence and cynicism of this very well in his imperishable treatise *The Enchanted Glass*, but let me borrow a brief summary from him because it shows the working of Bagehotian calculation in the distillation of primitive magic.

In 1911, the United Kingdom was in three kinds of trouble. Ireland was menaced by Republican and Loyalist insurrection, the modern Labour movement was emerging in a series of sharp-fought

22

engagements and the whole fabric and patina of Victorian family precept was being challenged by the immodest conduct of the women's suffrage movement. David Lloyd George, for whom that phrase 'a downy old bird with a good eye for cover' might have been invented, decided on a carnival of national unity, decked out in the finery of glamour and pageantry.

Nobody really knew what an 'Investiture' was supposed to look or sound or even feel like, but Lloyd George was too good an impresario to be deterred by that. As the then Prince of Wales, later Edward VIII, Duke of Windsor and putative Nazi collaborator, recalled in his own memoirs, he was compelled to be attended by a tailor, who had been commissioned to make: 'a fantastic costume designed for the occasion, consisting of white satin breeches and a mantle and surcoat of purple velvet edged with ermine'. In his acute embarrassment at this appalling rig, the Prince made an accidental obeisance to authenticity: 'I had already submitted to the Garter dress and robe, *for which there existed a condoning historical precedent . . .*' (italics mine). In other words, all parties to the show knew that the exercise was a deceitful one; an early prefiguration of the 'Heritage Britain' of *kitsch* history that has now come upon us. By the time the present Prince of Wales was taken by his mother to Caernarvon and 'presented' to the joyful people of the Principality, there already was a 'condoning historical precedent' in the shape of Lloyd George's stop-gap opportunism. This precedent was lovingly followed in 1969, with the awkward Charles being taught to mouth some Welsh phrases even as his unhappy ancestor had mugged them up with a silver-tongued Welsh solicitor as his tutor. There was one unambiguously good result of this humiliation for Edward, Prince of Wales. He got on better terms with the man who, as he wrote, 'only a few years before had shocked my family with his famous Limehouse speech attacking inherited privilege.' I suspect that it is this kind of reconciliation that the partisans of monarchy have in mind when they intone about blessed 'continuity'. Precedent, after all, connotes precedence.

There is a mysterious word that keeps coming up when pageantry and glamour are being extolled. The word is 'sacral'. It is hovering in the air as young Edward describes his 'Investiture':

> Upon my head he put the coronet cap as a token of principality, and into my hand the gold verge of government, and on my middle finger the gold ring of responsibility.

None of which, by 1936, were to do him any good. But it is not easy to profane such flummery in the face of simple, absolute, refusal to learn from history. At the coronation of the present Queen, *The Times* had an editorial which actually did say:

Today's sublime ceremonial is in form, and in common view, a dedication of the State to God's service through the prayers and benedictions of the Church. That is a noble conception, and of itself makes every man and woman in the land a partaker in the mystery of the Queen's anointing. But the Queen also stands for the soul as well as for the body of the Commonwealth. In her is incarnate on her Coronation the whole of society, of which the State is no more than a political manifestation.

This aspect of matters is integral to the pageantry and glamour. The 'sacral' moment or, as it is sometimes described, the moment of 'sacring', is as near to the divine right principle as we dare to get. The official guide to the ceremony dissolves in contradiction here, because it says of the sacral moment that it comes from Zadok the priest, who anointed Solomon as King of the Jews, *and* that the ceremony follows the old Saxon ritual, *and* that the moment is to be accompanied by the singing of Handel. The Saxons had no Handel, the British monarch must swear to uphold the Protestant faith, and so on and so on, but let it pass, lest the magic be unavailing. My point is that the word 'sacral' derives from the sacrum, the triangular bone that shields the back of the pelvis. Known to the ancients as the *os sacrum* or sacred bone, it has a common root with 'sacrifice'. In other words, in this bit of preserved bone-worship, one is not exaggerating the use of the word 'fetishism'.

'Glamour and pageantry', then, turn out to be *either* recent theatre *or* timeless witchcraft, or some politicised combination of the two. This, one feels, would be perfectly evident to the British if they saw it being manifested in another culture. It is the sort of man-worship and paganism that we told ourselves we went to India and Africa to cure, if the old history books are giving a true account. It is the sort of flirtation with idolatry that belongs to the early childhood of the human race. Except in our case, of course.

It also has one unmistakeable contemporary consequence. The Queen and her successors are bound to uphold the Protestant ascendancy *as a condition of legitimacy*. They must swear at their accession that they are not secret Catholics, they must forswear marriage to any man or woman of that faith and they must, at the 'sacring', renew the oath of a religious sect. How healthy is this for a society with a secular majority and large Roman Catholic, Jewish and Muslim minorities? Religious ideas, supposedly private matters between man and god, are in practice always political ideas. Our Sovereign Lady the Queen is the guarantor of only one of the confessions followed by her many subjects (so perhaps it's now a relief that she is no longer, as she was when 'anointed', the Queen of South Africa and Pakistan). To the many charges against monarchy we should add that in the British case it negates the separation of Church and State, one of the greatest gains of the Enlightenment, and that it does so, furthermore, by demonstrating partiality for one temporal church. The present state of affairs in Ulster, consecrated by the 'Glorious Revolution', may not in the longer run be the worst example of this unwisdom.

3. The Royal Family does not interfere in, but only lends tone to politics To this often-repeated incantation, there are two responses. The first could be called metaphorical, and would derive in part from the answers to the assertion posed above. It is a paltry definition of a nation's 'political' life that excludes the customary, the tribal, the ritualistic and the commemorative. One suspects that those who ignore this obvious point are doing so deliberately, in order to fend off blasphemy or any unauthorised glimpse of the sepulchre.

The second response is more direct and specific. Not only *is* the monarchy a powerful symbolic intervention into politics and government, but it conducts and has always conducted very deliberate interventions of a more tangible sort. To assert the obvious here is to encounter another difficulty in the tautology and contradiction department, because the monarchist faction are protean and slippery. They do not deny now (though they did then) the improper influence of Queen Victoria on Cabinets and Prime Ministers. They do not deny now (though they did then) the occasional startling exercise of Palace power during later reigns. The diaries of the present Queen's equerries and secretaries, if the state does not employ the royal prerogative to suppress them, will likewise contain many enlightening episodes. The odd difficulty lies in getting people to admit, not that it has happened or even will happen, but that it *does* happen or even that it *could* happen. Such is the hold of myth.

Let us compromise and take the genial case of King George V, the most typically avuncular/paternal of recent monarchs – once known as 'the National Dad' – and a man of no violent prejudice or temperament. We know of a series of vital decisions in which he exerted the influence of his kingship.

At about the time of the phoney 'Investiture' of the Prince of Wales, amid the turmoil of liberal England's strange death, King George V's principal private secretary, Lord Stamfordham, wrote to Home Secretary Reginald McKenna. The letter made a very definite suggestion that the government practice of force-feeding suffragette prisoners like Mrs Pankhurst should be discontinued. It made a clear allusion to forthcoming legislation and asked that it be changed. Even though it was couched in high Establishment terms ('Her story will horrify people otherwise not in sympathy with the Militant Suffragettes') the import of the letter was impossible to mistake, and contributed to the amendment of the infamous 'cat and mouse' policy.

A few years later, King George was engaged in another vital disagreement with 'His' ministry. He had been a friend of General Douglas Haig's, and could not believe that this gallant and agreeable officer (who was married to one of the Queen's maids of honour) was culpable for the calamities in Flanders. When Lloyd George, who certainly understood the influence of monarchy, tried to demote and control Haig, there was hell to pay. Haig openly appealed to the Palace. As the discredited general was later to note in his private journal:

> The King ... stated that he would 'support me through thick and thin' but I must be careful not to resign, because Lloyd George would then appeal to the country for support and would probably come back with a great majority ... The King's position would then be very difficult.

A number of later memoirs have since fleshed out this story of private alliance between a senior soldier and the King against the elected government. Again, the issue is not history's judgement of Haig as a general and later Field Marshal, nor even the astounding number of incised, lapidary names which testify to his and his king's qualities in every market square in the land. The issue is the role of the monarchy in making itself felt.

Shift the scene to 1931, when the abysmal

'National Government' was formed by Ramsay MacDonald, Stanley Baldwin and Sir Herbert Samuel. The chairman of the relevant meetings, all of them held behind closed doors, which inaugurated this hybrid regime was – King George V. Some authorities of the time held that he had violated even the unwritten elements of the constitution by the activism of his role; others maintained that he was trying to help an embattled Prime Minister as he was duty bound to do, but the fact remains that a new government was thereby formed and announced and that the first that the members of Parliament heard of it was on the radio.

In one case, that of the suffragettes, many would hail the King's humane concern. In the second case, that of the protection of Haig from the consequence of his folly, few would be so lenient. In the third case, it would have been easier to argue then than it would be to argue now that the King was 'simply' a peacemaker between factions and the patron of national consensus. Never mind the prejudices or preferences that were served by each intervention. The problem lies with those who say that such intervention does not occur, or does not amount to more than an informal touch on the tiller.

Two further examples may be useful. In July 1945 King George VI told Clement Attlee in round terms not to appoint Hugh Dalton as Foreign Secretary. He went further, and said who he thought *should* be appointed. His nominee, Ernest Bevin, got the post. Who would argue that this made no difference? Preferable, possibly. Irrelevant, hardly. Or we may consult the most recent and most informed study of the career of Harold Macmillan. After a disastrous war on Egypt which he had strongly urged upon the Cabinet, Macmillan found to his astonishment that his advice as followed had had the effect of driving Sir Anthony Eden round the bend. A new Prime Minister was needed in a hurry, in order to restore calm relations with 'allies' and tranquillity at home. I leave the denouement to Alistair Horne, principal and sympathetic chronicler. He first quotes Macmillan directly:

> He [Eden] told me with simple gravity, as a matter decided and not to be discussed, that he had decided to resign his office. The Queen had already been informed . . .

Next to be told after the Royal *fait accompli* came the Cabinet, who were according to Macmillan 'dazed' (though not at being told second). Then came the meeting of the Marquis of Salisbury and Lord Kilmuir, both of them Lords Temporal, who invited Ministers to call on them in the suggestively-named Privy Council offices. After a canvass of opinion for which they did not have to account to anybody, they must have said something to somebody because, in Horne's words:

The next morning Macmillan waited in lonely isolation under a portrait of Gladstone in No. 11, and 'read *Pride and Prejudice* – very soothing. At noon Sir Michael Adeane rang up and asked me to be at the Palace at two o'clock. So it was settled . . .'

So indeed it was. When Macmillan caved in a number of years later as a result of a concatenation of scandals, his succession was arranged in such a neo-Byzantine fashion that it led to a reform of the Tory Party's innermost councils and was denounced by a senior Conservative as the operation of a 'magic circle'. But, as in old Byzantium, the fault was only to be found in the sovereign's advisors and courtiers, never in the sacred person, let alone in the fact of a mystical sovereignty. The classic, servile reservation ('I don't much care for some of the hangers-on') has become a satirical byword in our time because of those who lamented that Stalin and Mao were 'poorly advised'. But servility is servility the whole world over. It is just that in Britain it takes a royalist shape. This brings us conveniently to objection (4) which is:

4. The Royal Family is preferable to the caprices of presidential government How easy it is to see the ground of this point. The United States, for example, has never had a President quite as bad as King George III, but neither has Britain had a king as admirable as George Washington (of whom William Thackeray rightly said that 'his glory will descend to remotest ages' while the memory of the sovereign went the other way). Still, even to concede this obvious argument is to make it plain that a bad monarch is *at least* as likely as a bad president even given the caprice of random selection by the hereditary principle.

But if we take the most obvious parallel or comparison, which is that of the United States, what do we find? We find that the presidency has become too secretive, too powerful, too trammelled, too ceremonial, too impotent or too complicated, depending on the president under discussion or the critic making the analysis. On one thing all are agreed – there is a danger of an 'imperial' or 'monarchical' presidency. An incumbent in Washington knows he is in trouble on the day that cartoonists begin to represent him as a king.

A peculiarity of the recent past is that the contrast, if it is a contrast, between a serene head of state and a fierce and determined head of government has actually increased royalist sympathy in the most unexpected quarters. Informed whispers in well-connected liberal circles disclose to us that the Queen is not amused by the Prime Minister's attitude towards her former dominion of South Africa, for example, or towards her less advantaged subjects. This may or may not be true – the evidence is that on 'Commonwealth' questions Her Majesty reserves a certain autonomy when it comes to the expression of an opinion. But you can't have it both ways. Queen Victoria used to browbeat poor Mr Gladstone most dreadfully when it came to overseas or, as they were then called, 'imperial' matters. Either this is proper or it isn't. You either accept the principle of royal intervention or you don't. And if you don't, you always have the choice of an actual 'Commonwealth' – the beautiful and resonant name given by the English revolutionaries to the most forbidden passage of our history after the removal of the Stuarts. What would Milton have said of a culture where even the republicans were vying for royal attention?

This in turn raises the last and in many ways the most essential question, which is also contained in objection (5).

5. The Royal Family is a guarantee of the national 'identity' This can only be true for a person who sincerely believes it, and we know that there are people for whom the country and a certain rather mediocre dynasty are in effect unimaginable without one another. There is no need to doubt or mock the sincerity of the conviction. However, there is no reason in our history or our literature to endorse or underwrite it either. We possess an alternative tradition which is capable of outlasting this royal house as it has already outlasted others.

Consider, for a start, the celebrated editorial

which appeared in *The Times* on the occasion of the death of George IV in 1830. The article mentioned the deposition of the late king's wife by a 'fashionable strumpet', touched on his early debaucheries in a seasoned manner and said, almost exaggerating the facts of the case:

> There never was an individual less regretted by his fellow-creatures than this deceased King. What eye has wept for him? What heart has heaved one sob of unmercenary sorrow?

The nearest to a forgiving remark that the editorialist achieved in the remainder of the obituary was to describe the departed monarch with a touch of irony as 'that Leviathan of *haut ton*'. Again, never mind the correctness or otherwise of the opinion. If grim death were (heaven forfend) to overtake Prince Philip tomorrow, it would not matter whether *The Times* and the rest of them *thought* ill of him. They would never dare to *say* as much. So, whatever our current awe, discretion and unction may claim for itself, it cannot decently claim to be part of a sturdy, confident English tradition.

Is there in fact such a thing as a sturdy, confident English tradition? There is, at any rate, a very solid and honourable Republican tradition, which ought not to be covered by fawning velvet drapes. We are not descended from a past when the institution of monarchy was uncritically accepted, though there were times when men and women preferred to fight over which monarch it should be, rather than whether to have a monarch at all. Even when such was the case, or when thinkers and teachers were no more audacious than to argue what kind of *kingship* was preferable, there was more debate and disputation than there is now. Locke, for example, ridiculed Hobbes for believing that a sovereign arose in nature to enforce a contract to which he was not himself a party:

> As if when men, quitting the state of Nature, entered into Society, they agreed that all of them but one should be under the restraint of laws; but that he should still retain all the liberty of the state of Nature, increased with power, and made licentious by impunity. This is to think that men are so foolish that they take care to avoid what mischiefs may be done them by polecats or foxes, but are content, nay think it safety, to be devoured by lions.

Locke was making a rod for his own back by this argument, since he was a partisan of the Glorious Revolution and the enthronement of William and Mary. His case against Hobbes's version of absolutism was partial, in both senses of the word. But its implications were less so. At least Hobbes and Locke could ply their trade in the relatively sane interlude between the slavishness of divine right and the prestidigitation of Bagehot and his emulators.

The extraordinary Thomas Paine was to become the first general theorist of republicanism, transcending the rather narrowly Puritan anti-monarchists of the English Revolution and proposing a state where, as he put it with some warmth and emphasis: THE LAW IS KING. In today's Britain, the idea that there could be a Constitution more powerful – and even sacrosanct – than any crowned head or elected politician (thus abolishing the false antithesis between hereditary monarchs and capricious presidents) is thought of as a breathtakingly new and daring idea. But even in the most corrupted period of 1970s America it was found simple enough as a scheme, and as a principle, to put an end to the tenure of a twice-elected and still popular President.

Milton, Bunyan, Shelley, Blake, Thackeray, Dilke, Russell, Harrison – not all of these were Republicans *tout court* but all were prepared to denounce a monarch or to satirise the institution. They were free-thinking and ambitious men, who could not be persuaded that happiness depended upon man-made illusions. Some of them also wrote rather better poetry than the Laureate Alfred Austin, say, whose immortal lines:

Over the wires the electric message came –
He is no better, he is much the same

were written for the outpouring of sickly national concern that surrounded the illness of the afore-mentioned Prince of Wales in 1871. So what can one say of Ted Hughes, who seems not to have realised what he was borrowing from Locke in the following stanza written for the Queen Mum's birthday in 1985:

It was an eerie vision! The Land of the Lion!
Each clear creature, crystal-bright,
Honey-lit with lion-light,
All dreaming together the Dream of the Lion.

Oh, for Christ's *sake*. If nothing else, could we not cease to disfigure our poetic tradition by at least abolishing the Laureateship? Probably not, for as Hughes goes on to imply, the whole thing is one bally seamless garment:

. . . But now the globe's light hardens. The
    dreams go.
And what is so is so.
The awakened lands look bare.
A Queen's life is hard. Yet a Queen reigns
Over the dream of her people, or nowhere.

Probably true, that last line. And the penultimate line condenses one of the all-time favourite saloon-bar loyalist clichés: '*I* wouldn't have her job'. Those who profess unquenchable love for the sovereign

38

are adamant that she press on in a task that they consider killingly hard. Sir James Frazer, chronicler in *The Golden Bough* of the connection between kingship and symbolic murder, would probably have been able to analyse this moist tribute from first principles.

As I tried to argue at the outset, there is a slightly sinister resemblance between the vicarious and redemptive duties that we heap upon the emblem and the person of monarchy, and the fanatical trust that is placed in clerical or religious or shamanistic salvation in 'other' cultures. Most developed societies found out the essential way to handle politics and religion a long time ago. Seeing what happened when a compromise between the two was *not* adopted, they went for the obvious solution. Keep them apart. Humans should not worship other humans at all, but if they must do so it is better that the worshipped ones do not occupy any positions of political power. We had another chance to contemplate the alternative as recently as 1989, when the Emperor Hirohito finally expired. It was generally if rather unenthusiastically agreed that he had atoned for his past, that he had had 'no real power' where Japanese militarism and racialism were concerned, that, although he was a god, he had been a 'mere figurehead' and – so that no aspect of the argument from credulity should be spared us – that he has used *such power as he had enjoyed* to restrain his murderous junta. It was not uncommon to see the same person arguing all these things on the same obituary programme. But by what right do we smile at the slavish leader-cult of the Japanese when we too believe that we have a demi-divine family that has no power except an enormous one, and that exclusively exercised for the common good?

Too many crucial things about this country turn out to be highly recommended because they are 'invisible'. There is the 'hidden hand' of the free market, the 'unwritten' Constitution, the 'invisible earnings' of the financial service sector, the 'magic' of monarchy and the 'mystery' of the Church and its claim to the interpretation of revealed truth. When we do get as far as the visible or the palpable, too much of it is deemed secret. How right it is that senior ministers, having kissed hands with the monarch, are sworn to the cult of secrecy by 'The Privy Council Oath'. How right it is that our major foreign alliance – the 'special relationship' with the United States – is codified by no known treaty and regulated by no known Parliamentary instrument.

Yet those who govern us as if we were infants expect us to be grateful that at least we live in 'a family'; a family, moreover, patterned on the ideal by the example of the Windsors. A beaming gran, a dutiful mum, a stern and disciplined father, and children who are . . . well, all analogies based upon family break down somewhere. The analogy between family and society, as it happens, breaks down as soon as it is applied. The 'United Kingdom' is not a family and never was one. (Not even Orwell, with his image of poor relations, rich relations and 'the wrong members in control', could make it stick.) It is a painfully evolved society, at once highly stratified and uniform and very fluid and diverse, which is the site of a multitude of competing interests. Other states in the past sought to conceal this truth from themselves by the exercise of projection – customarily onto a dynasty with supposedly extraordinary powers of healing and unification. This did not save them: indeed historians usually attribute part of the magnitude of the eventual smash to the ingrained, faithful, fatalistic fixation. The supplanting of monarchy, in those circumstances, by new forms of despotism was not the negation of monarchy but the *replication* of it by societies not yet cured of the addiction.

There have, as we know from *1066 and All That* and from the more recent experience of Juan Carlos of Spain and Emperor Bokassa, been 'good kings' and 'bad kings'. But need we depend upon such whimsy at all? Right before us is the respectable alternative of a Constitution, which is indeed enshrined above the Law but only to keep Law in order. This is a safeguard against any impulse, either of the *ad hoc* or the idealistic variety, to treat human beings as political property. Thomas Paine, chivvied out of England by royal police spies, contrived to transplant this idea to America and to depose, at least in the Thirteen Colonies, the man who had exiled him. Paine's later emulators have striven in great democratic battles for the essential idea that we should be *citizens* not *subjects*.

In their last ditch, the royalists object that this is all too bloodless and practical; that people need and want the element of magic and fantasy. Nobody wants life to be charmless. But the element of fantasy and magic is as primitive as it is authentic, and there are good reasons why *it should not come from the state*. When orchestrated and distributed in that way, it leads to disappointment and rancour, and can lead to the enthronement of sillier or nastier idols.

Is this an argument for abolition? Of course it is. But not for an abolition by fiat: for yet another political change that would come as a surprise to the passively governed. It is an invitation to think – are you serious when you say that you cannot imagine life without it? Do you *prefer* invented tradition, sanitised history, prettified literature, state-sponsored superstition and media-dominated pulses of cheering and jeering? A people that began to think as citizens rather than subjects might transcend underdevelopment on their own. Inalienable human right is unique in that it needs no superhuman guarantee; no 'fount' except itself. Only servility requires the realm (suggestive word) of illusion. Illusions, of course, cannot be abolished. But they can and must be outgrown.

About the Author

CHRISTOPHER HITCHENS lives in Washington D.C., where he is a columnist for *Harper's* and *The Nation* and a book critic for *New York Newsday*. He has been the American columnist for *The Spectator*, *The New Statesman* and the *Times Literary Supplement*. His books include *Karl Marx and the Paris Commune*, *James Callaghan: The Road to Number Ten* (with Peter Kellner), *Cyprus*, *The Elgin Marbles*, *Blaming the Victims* (with Edward Said) and *Prepared for the Worst*.

CHATTO
CounterBlasts

Also available in bookshops now:-

Forthcoming Chatto CounterBlasts

Plus pamphlets from Michael Holroyd, Hanif Kureishi, Michael Ignatieff and Susannah Clapp

If you want to join in the debate, and if you want to know more about **CounterBlasts**, the writers and the issues, then write to:

Random House UK Ltd, Freepost 5066, Dept MH, London WC1B 3BR